Messages from a Mystic Traveler

A Memoir By

Michael Williams

Brighter Lights Publishing—Staten Island, NY
ISBN: 979-8-9862972-4-8
Library of Congress Control Number: pending
Title: *Messages from a Mystic Traveler*
Author: Michael Williams
Digital distribution | 2022
Paperback | 2022

Disclaimer

I have tried to recreate events, locales and descriptions from my memories of them. Some names and identifying details have been omitted to protect the privacy of individuals. This book is not intended as a substitute for the medical advice of physicians. The reader should regularly consult a physician in matters relating to health, and particularly with respect to any symptoms that may require diagnosis or medical attention.

Dedication

I dedicate this book to those explorers who seek spiritual or mystical understanding in our world.

Preface

At the funeral for my father, surrounded by family and friends, I revealed something many of them did not know, a side of me that was kept secret, that is mystical and spiritual. I spoke to the small crowd about a brief spiritual experience with my father upon his exit from this world. At the end of the funeral, as we were walking to our cars, a relative stopped me for a moment to recommend a book about spirituality. Her motive to share the name of this book was probably triggered by the spiritual encounter that I shared with the guests at this ceremony. After she recommended the title, I remember telling her that I did not need to read about this subject, that I could write a book myself.

I will be taking you on a journey to a world that we do not always have access to, to a destination that is not always defined, a place that is a mystery to most of us.

Chapter One

Many of us know that although we cannot see the multitude of bacteria or viruses with the human eye in this reality, they do exist. Through human ingenuity we are able to observe these life forms in action. Before the invention of microscopic tools, people had to guess why certain individuals became ill. There were some crazy ideas to solve these afflictions. One of these was draining blood from the body using leeches. In modern times we have discovered that some microorganisms are problematic, and have developed reasonable methods to deal with them. What if we share another kind of world unseen by our eyes? This world is similar in concept to microscopic life, a reality actively around us, affecting us, yet no modern tool has been invented to view it.

What if you had a vision while sleeping? Would you likely go about your day thinking it was only a dream? What if you encountered these images and events in your dreams later in life, in the reality in which we live now, and you witnessed these scenes two weeks later, three months, or years later? Furthermore, what if you awoke from a vivid sequence of images or a nightmare, and knew that scene seemed more real than the others? Would you wonder if that dream was real, a bad dream, or some random images from a scary movie you watched the night before?

I will be sharing some of my visions with you. These visions have not occurred often. There were gaps of possibly years before seeing another, and most are in the form of a dream. The images in these visions could be mystical, spiritual and sometimes raw. At times, they are entertaining, erotic, insightful, with a few potentially helpful in living our lives.

I recall having had spiritual experiences from as far back as early childhood. After years of research and self-discovery, I can say with confidence that I have mystical qualities. What my relative said at the funeral for my father inspired me to remember memories that had been long hidden, waiting until the right time to share. You will be exploring and discovering the possibilities with me.

Chapter Two
Spirituality 101

Spirits communicate by feeling. There have been a few spirits from whom I have heard a voice. I cannot be sure whether they used an actual voice, or whether the feeling communicated to me from these spirits was processed by my mind, then put into words that I could understand.

Many of us have encountered a spirit who tried to communicate with them. If you and a family member, or a person you are familiar with, have had a feeling that only the both of you have shared, there is a possibility that this sensation could be communicated to you later in life. When a spirit is sending you a message, that individual you have known who is now in spiritual form, could transmit that emotional energy that was specifically known to both of you. This kind of feeling could leave you with no doubt about who the sender is. The emotion could be love, a taste, a smell, a chill or some other sensation. You could have a sudden revelation, stopping yourself for a moment, thinking the feeling that just occurred was strange, but on another level have a personal understanding that there is something more to that. Your senses could be telling you that this sensation is from someone you know, who is now in their spirit form. Furthermore, you may realize that in this brief encounter, this message is from your mother, father, uncle, or possibly a relative trying to comfort you during a difficult time; this entity is probably someone you had a bond with or were close to.

Spirits have the same feelings as we do, and depending on their emotional state, appear in various colors. Whether you are asleep or awake, all spirits are seen as energy. That energy appears with shape and colors. Angry spirits may look red and sometimes disorganized, while spirits who look stable and content may have more definition and organization. Some are represented as circles while others look similar to a small sparkle of energy.

Since all of us have a spirit, and the human body is their host, I believe that the mind has adapted to process spiritual energy, letting the human side of us recognize or understand these images or emotions. Thousands of years ago many people were more receptive or in tune with these spiritual energies. Long ago, we did not have all the distractions of today, all those thoughts that could cloud our vision or block our spiritual side. During that occasional moment we thought we felt something spiritual, in that short time, we may have communicated with a spirit. Our ancestors may not have thought of these spiritual experiences as strange; perhaps they were common in their time.

As a child, seeing spirits did not seem strange. What seemed awkward was reporting those sightings to adults. When you are told what is good, bad or indifferent, your mind must filter through all those norms or rules. Much of our education and filtering are needed for survival and acceptance, but if that out-of-the-ordinary experience does not fit into the normal state of the mind or standards of society, there could be side effects. A person could be criticized, become confused, have doubts, and in that loss of understanding feel agitated, and detract from this kind of ability. Although any person is at risk for criticism when sharing a spiritual encounter, I recommend we use and accept our senses/feelings. Like the air, they are still free.

Chapter Three
Arrival

There are memories that were never meant to be forgotten. A mother or father may say that memory was the first time their child said, "Daddy" or "Mommy." Do you remember the first memory in your lifetime?

My first memory in this world started with a large surge of energy, as if an electric light were clicked on, as I became conscious, looking through new eyes. I knew I was in a body, then looked down to see whether I was a boy or girl. After a few seconds of looking down, I discovered I was a boy. I did not want to be a girl and was very happy about being in a male body. A voice in my mind said, "Thank God."

Then I looked up at the sky, and there was a clear, watery, round image, with an extremely strong energy—part of me was in awe of how strong that energy felt. I thought for a second, should I say something out loud, then decided to say thank you with feeling instead. I directed my feeling energy, positive energy, towards this image in the sky. After this powerful entity recognized my gesture, he felt admiration and concern for me; then I sensed something else: he was in a hurry to go; then he disappeared.

Looking around, I guessed the house I was standing in front of was where I belonged. I walked up the sidewalk and then the stairs. The woman inside the home called me Michael. I found out later that I was her son. I felt awkward/vulnerable being in the body of a child of about four years old. Part of me was annoyed that people were treating me like a child.

I scanned in every direction the world I was in, and had a bad feeling. When I think back, at the time there were wars in certain parts of the globe, but this was a general feeling, a non-specific feeling that could not be defined in words. Besides, I was somewhat annoyed my spirit was woken up. With that first jolt of energy, I found myself awake in this reality, in the body of a little boy.

I have encountered spirits with either a male or female voice, observing the possibility that a spirit may identify more with being either gender. There is no insult intended or implied in being one or the other sex, a spirit may desire or gravitate towards being a man or woman upon arrival into this reality.

Chapter Four
The Observer

One of my first observations in this world was at about the age of five or six. I was standing outside near my home, when I heard a loud noise above. I looked up to see a very large object crossing the sky. The object looked very heavy, apparently a large flying machine. I remember saying to myself, "They've come a long way."

There was a small feeling of comparing something—from a different time.

An old soul can sometimes discover certain qualities in themselves, such as wisdom, artistic or musical ability, or an approach to life.

I found out later that the large object in the sky was a 747 jumbo-jet; that was my first time seeing one of the many technical marvels of human invention.

I have always been interested in seeing how people treat one another and interact. Sometimes I watch the media news, not always accepting their views or propaganda; observing the media to see what they are feeding their viewers, and consider how the audience could possibly behave, that is after digesting that content. If creative, the media can influence a person to wave a flag or to march in agreement or disagreement with almost any idea. I have always had this feeling that to understand this world, a person needs to seek experience and interact on some levels.

If you think about it, you are an observer, a participant and witness to a shared reality/future.

You are joining me in witnessing this reality (as an observer); as we focus in on this world today, we are observing a man-made climate crisis; Australia, California, the Amazon and other parts of this world have experienced extreme wildfires; the seas are dying; there have been many wars; starvation; floods; pandemics; destruction of ecosystems; plastics pollution; a mental health crisis; mass shootings; sea levels displacing human life; anti-Semitism; fascism; species going extinct; super-hurricanes and typhoons. There are likely more challenges to observe, for human life to unite and overcome.

Chapter Five
Time

With any prevailing currents, shortly after an event occurs, energy goes in all directions.

When I was about twelve years old, I was wondering how it was possible to see images of places while sleeping, then see those same locations weeks or months later. I was seeking to understand this concept, and another, how time could affect us.

I was walking through a forest with which I was familiar, thinking about time, when I was drawn to a lake. After walking to the edge of the water, I picked up a rock and threw it in. As the waves moved away from the impacting rock, there was the answer. The waves floating away from the center symbolized time as a wave of energy. A small rock thrown into the water created a small wave—representing a minor event or energy, and a larger wave from a bigger stone—represented a more significant wave or event.

Imagine you are standing in a lake, the water up to your waist. Your friend throws a small rock into the water. You may or may not feel on your skin the push of water coming from the resulting wave, but when your companion throws a much larger rock into the liquid, you cannot help but feel the sensation from the wave. When there is an event, the dropping of a rock into the water, the energy produced by that experience spreads out from the center to all directions. As with a radio frequency, if you are in tune to that radio wave, sensitive to it, you will receive or detect that information. The greater the energy coming from that frequency, the louder that station becomes or the longer the distance that energy travels.

If you think about a meteor crashing into the ground or a structure, the energy of that event travels in all directions. People in the area may feel the ground shake or hear a loud noise—that energy from its origin taking on different forms, traveling from its center.

What if that traumatic energy were felt in seconds or weeks before the event occurred? And what if someone living nearby had a strange feeling, or a premonition of danger? That person may be sensing the energy waves that represent that event in time.

I have sometimes seen time as a single unit, where the entire scope of time is a continuous entity. For instance, you could be in one city seeing that reality, while other people are seeing events, sharing the same time-line in other cities or locations. The energy around us is not governed by the rules of an invention called time. In a moment that is not measured, separated or calculated using the idea of time: the now, the past and the future are connected by the same energy, which consists of the physical reality, with all events occurring in that space.

Chapter Six
"You never know." (Something I can never say)

Sometimes I hear the words, "You never know" from people I am talking with, or in the media. In saying that, you could be programming or telling your mind not to know, creating a block, disabling your ability to use your intuition. Saying you never know could eliminate any possibly that you do know something that could benefit you or the people around you.

I once told a friend: "If I cannot get on an airplane, and cannot explain the reason, please do not get onboard."

I have read about or watched stories where people have had a strange feeling of doom before entering into a situation. Note that there is a possibility those same people who listened and acted upon that strange/unfamiliar feeling or intuition are likely still here today, a survivor who somehow knew. This person probably did not stop to ask why, or hold back that feeling back by saying, I never know; that critical information/intuition if not overlooked, could potentially result in a positive outcome. That is why I never say, "You never know."

Chapter Seven
Antenna

I was taking a college course in the 1980s when the instructor directed an off-topic question to the class. He asked why a church has a tower? No one raised their hand to answer. Then I thought, this question is easy. I raised my hand up and the teacher said, "Go ahead."

I answered, "The tower is an antenna to God."

The tower or spire on most religious buildings appear higher than the rest of the structure. Whether they are a beacon to alert people to the presence of a temple or church from afar, there must be another purpose. A television antenna is high enough to send or receive messages, a spiritual antenna could have a similar goal. Traveling through the tower, a collective payer or energy could be funneled towards the sky or heavens, or the hope is the antenna could receive a message from God or another spirit.

Chapter Eight
The Wrong Path?

After a few weeks in this body, I woke up one morning with a strong feeling that this day was special—that something big was going to happen. While I was standing outside in the front of the house where I was living, there was a gray car parked across the street. Then to the left of the car, near the front, stood a beautiful blonde woman with blue eyes. All of a sudden, in my mind I heard a voice say, "Your mother, talk to her." I stared at the woman for a few seconds, looking into her eyes; she almost seemed startled that I was looking directly into her eyes. In that moment I thought, "What do I say?" Being in a very strange situation, and not understanding what was going on, I decided to go back into the house. As I sat on a chair near the window, I could see she was still standing outside waiting for me. In that state of mind of being very unsure, I had a feeling that God would soon talk to me.

Suddenly, a spirit was there, and he said, "Talk to her."

Then when I would not move, the spirit said, "He will be alright." As quickly as that spirit came, he was gone. I looked outside, the woman was gone, and in that moment, I had a vision of a new path or life— that there was a shift in time.

The day after seeing the woman outside the house, I thought maybe I should have listened to the spirit and talked to her. A few minutes later, I walked down the street where I lived to find a quiet place to think about the day before. As I was walking, I stopped, looked up at the sky, and said, "Why am I here?"

A spirit appeared in the clear blue sky, in an annoyed female voice she said, "To live a life."

Then I said, "How can I talk to you again?"

She said, "Don't talk." After a few seconds, she said, "Don't trust anyone."

After that day, I always remembered the advice about not talking, to keep my mind as quiet as possible, and by eliminating the mental chatter, that this cleared the mind—I learned later people called this technique meditation.

Finding a place to sit down alone, I thought about what to do next. I had a vision of a building with scaffolding located in an urban area. Remembering that I had ridden on a train some time before that day, and that I had seen a sign with a city name on it, I thought about taking a train ride to find the woman from the day before. But this idea would not be realized, because I was in the body of a little boy around the age of five. I gave up on the idea of taking the train by myself at this very young age; I would be held by the authorities, and my parents would be called, and asked why I was traveling alone. I finally thought about how to deal with the uncertainty. I decided to live the best life possible, knowing perhaps, my memory of those events outside the house the day before, put my life in the wrong direction.

Chapter Nine
The Block

When I was about age seven, my parents decided to move to a safer neighborhood. As I reflected on my time living in an unsafe area, I had no trouble leaving some of these memories behind. I was living in the very small body of a child during the late 1960s. I was never prejudiced, but a small boy in an atmosphere of racial riots and class warfare could obviously be harmed—I lived in fear, and was already uncomfortable living as a child. Every day, I wondered when I would be beaten up or have my money stolen. Being in a small body did not help; any bigger child no matter his race could prey on me. At the time, there was positive news, my mother announced we were moving, and I was delighted, maybe I would not have to live in fear.

Before relocating to a new home, I reviewed my current inventory of experiences and decided that I had to protect myself from some harmful or confusing memories. I decided that wondering about that woman outside the house, as well as some of the other spiritual experiences, and the abuse suffered as a small child, would not be productive in moving forward. In thinking that those memories could do more harm than good produced another idea: why not block them until I was old enough to understand them better? With that in mind, I put a memory block upon myself, to protect my very young fragile life going forward in the world.

While creating the block a number mysteriously came to mind, "52." I would not remember those memories until age 52—the block was put into effect. There were two memories or names that I felt were important enough to recall, to not block them. They were meeting a spirit named "God" and a woman who may have had some kind of influence on my life. I realized later, in doing that, I may have blocked other important memories or abilities about myself, subsequently leading to other challenges. In not knowing my full potential, or blocking that knowledge/ability, I was not prepared for what might come next. I did not understand then there was not only a physical strength, but a kind of spiritual strength that I may not have fully understood, that having a block could have possibly kept that ability hidden.

At age 52, like a flood, my childhood memories were unblocked and started to come back.

Chapter Ten
Lightning without Thunder or Rain

I was a teenager, and one night had a vision while sleeping. In the vision, I was looking into the darkness at a beach, and beyond that, I could see a lighthouse. I was feeling a very powerful energy; my senses were telling me to stay alert, something was about to happen. Above the lighthouse, out of the clear night sky, lightning bolts were dropping down onto the water around the tiny circular building. As I observed the bolts of energy streaming down, I noticed the absence of thunder and rain. I sensed it was time to go, that I was near an angry spirit. I do not know why I felt that somebody was being judged, but thought it best not to be in the path of this spirit.

As the images progressed, I found myself seeing a dark forest. There was a sense of urgency. I could see people on my left and right, moving towards something or somebody. There was a chase, and I could sense the person on the run had broken some type of rule—perhaps something spiritual. That he may have used his special ability to cause harm. I did not know what he did, or what power he may have used, but he was now in the domain of a very angry spirit. He crossed some type of line, or defied some kind of moral code, that found him in deep trouble. At the time, I was not focusing on whether he violated some kind of trust or broke a law, I sensed the utter urgency. There was no time to rationalize this situation, I was in the presence of this very powerful spirit. I did not want to be in the middle of the chase, or in the path of a possible judgment. I decided at that moment to leave the area and the vision ended.

The next day, a girl invited me to a beach where there would be a party. I accepted, and while at the party during the daytime, I had an ominous feeling it was time to leave. I said to her that I had a feeling it was going to rain. I did not say anything to her about what I felt, the vision I had the night before, or the foreboding feeling that I was being chased away.

Another day went by when I received a call from the woman I met at the beach. She said that after I left the party, there was a loud crack of thunder, then rain and lightning coming down from around the lighthouse a few miles away. She explained that there was not a cloud in the sky; that they were really unprepared for the rain pouring down all around them. She said that she thought it was lucky that I left when I did. Then she informed me about an article in the newspaper that day. A serial killer was captured during the night at the same beach where we met for the party; he was captured during a chase by authorities while running in the nearby forest.

Chapter Eleven
Media

I have watched and read several types of media. The corporate media/propaganda machine has a large influence on our understanding, if you choose to watch and digest it. In a typical local television news show, the first twenty minutes of the formula is negative programming, followed by some health reporting, a small good news story, the weather, then sports. If you think of the TV news programming as medicine, 70 to 80 percent of the dose is negative. Think about how that influences the average viewer's thinking and perception of our world.

The media influence on the nationality of a country is sometimes very evident. To all those people who wave a flag for their country, I commend you, you brave warriors. Most people would agree that an idea motivates patriotism, but what fuels it is human emotion—which is sometimes manipulated expertly by the media.

Chapter Twelve
Patriotism

In our world, the messages we receive affect our behaviors. Look at the man waving the flag for his country. At that moment, he thinks his country is great. He has taken into his mind ideas that have encouraged him to stand up in public to display his honor. Anyone else who is faithful to his cause will stand with him or praise his efforts, but history tells us about governments/empires. While I admire his patriotism, he may not understand that there have been many empires that have existed, and many people have cheered for their leader or nation. What we should note in history is that every empire has failed and/or expired, had a rise and then ultimately a fall. You may think of a kingdom like the weather: there were times when the skies were clear and pleasant, then a serious event or storm came along to wipe out that empire.

Being told that all empires have fallen could dampen the energy to raise a flag, be patriotic or rise to the occasion during a crisis. We should also know that governments are dynamic, changing with the cast of characters who populate them. As most know, anything can grow with time and effort, or sour if not maintained. As with any lifespan, an empire has a beginning and an end.

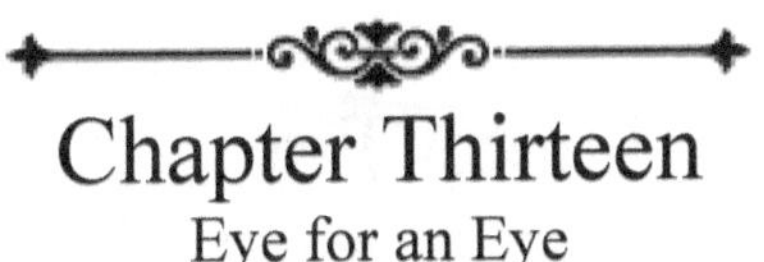

Chapter Thirteen
Eye for an Eye

Ever since being a young child, when somebody would hurt me, I would take the approach of an eye for an eye—if you hurt me, I would hurt you back. I did not always feel that I was in control of this emotion, as if it were already built-in.

In this modern world, an eye for an eye or revenge could be thought of as a double-edge sword. If you retaliate against that criminal suspect, you could hurt yourself in pursuit of that goal. This concept could be seen when a father wants to take revenge on a crime committed on his child. He goes to hurt or kill the suspect, is charged with a crime, has now hurt himself, his family and doubled or tripled his suffering.

Chapter Fourteen
Love (the most powerful energy)

Everyone has felt love in one way or another. When you have heard that melody of a love song that you are unable to stop playing in your mind, you are feeling some of that energy.

Love is the most powerful energy, and is universal—every species communicates this emotion in different languages or dances. Without this positive energy, most of us would not be living today. It is a powerful force that moves life forward.

Evidence of a break in this important force may be seen when a spouse dies. Sometimes that surviving person cannot live with that void, may become depressed, suffer other health problems, and perish sooner.

Love is an abused word. Somebody might say he loves a car, a bouquet of flowers, a song, a sunset, all kinds of things. Although the word love is sometimes associated with material objects or simple descriptions, many of us associate this emotion with romantic love.

The energy of love is the most powerful emotion, a creative force. In romantic love, the power of two individuals becomes a more significant force. The idea of divide and conquer does not operate well in the realm of love, because love brings people together; it is an energy that unites us. Love brings groups of individuals together: people who love working together are making something larger, a greater force with more relevance, a much larger collective energy to achieve more.

In our human form we have adapted to the biology of love, but a spiritual kind of love exists. When a person dies, the spirit can ask questions and see them answered. A female spirit might question whether she was truly loved by a certain person she cared about. Perhaps in her human form, she had some type of doubt, not enough proof in her mind that her significant other felt the same way.

Love is a powerful creative force, natural and needed for our survival. This positive energy is felt internally and externally, is spontaneous or learned, and if maintained builds on itself to evolve.

Chapter Fifteen
Anger (Negative Energy)

Anger/hate is a negative energy that comes in different forms. I have always viewed anger as having a burning effect, like a raging fire, and sometimes see this emotion as a red color. Of course, we all know fire burns and destroys things; negative energy may have the same effect. Anger corrupts the mind, motivates us to speak loudly, seek revenge, and ultimately may propel us to hurt ourselves or somebody else as a result.

If at all possible, anger and fear should be avoided. The reason is not always obvious to most of us. There are systems in the body and mind that react to this type of stress. In heightened emotionality, such as in the fight or flight response, our bodies react without our control to this stimulus—to help us function or survive. The purpose is mainly to get us out of risky situations. In the fight or flight response, blood flow is increased to our vital organs and slowed to our brain—this is to give the body the appropriate energy to run or fight. Have you ever wondered why when someone is very emotional, that person cannot process thoughts and is very tired? The anger, fear and panic emotions shunt blood to the brain. All that energy that could be used to slowly think things through is being redirected from the mind to the physical body to respond.

Fear, anger and worry deplete our energy, sometimes feeling more exhausting than running on a track. How far you go depends on the level of worry or anger. That prolonged emotion may have you saying, why am I so tired, what did I do?

Look at the situation in which there are two players on opposing sports teams. One player says something to the other player to get him angry, then that very annoyed player is unable to think straight, does something inappropriate, and receives a penalty. The angry player says to himself, what was I thinking?

Therefore, if in that split second you are able to ignore and not embrace negativity, you will find that your mind moves at a more even pace, reasoning flows slowly enough that you can see the road ahead, and think things through.

Chapter Sixteen
Missed by an Inch

I was walking across the median of a two-lane road, when I heard a female voice say, "You are going to die."

I thought, maybe I'm hearing things, and ignored it. The next week, I was walking across the same median and heard her again, "You are going to die."

I decided to respond to her by saying, "Miss by an inch."

Two weeks later, I was walking across the same two-lane road and sensed anger coming from a car; that vehicle was pointed in my direction. I do not know what the driver, a dark-haired person in his twenties was disturbed about, but I sensed he did not care what or who was in the way—the anger took over or corrupted his mind.

As he was recklessly driving at me, I moved away slightly to avoid him and at the same time, tried to be aware of the small space between myself and the opposite lane of traffic. I felt a rush of air go by me; he missed the left side of my body by an inch. As I looked at his car driving away, I could not help think, who or what drove this person to corrupt his mind with that much anger and/or recklessness?

Chapter Seventeen
Tunnel Vision

During the 1990s, I had a dream that took place in a tunnel. At first, the images looked exciting, a car traveling at high speed through a tunnel, but unfortunately there was a tragic end to this car ride.

There were two cars, one was chasing the other. In the car being chased, the passengers wanted to keep as far as possible, to get away from their pursuer. To achieve this goal, they decided to drive more quickly, and as their anxiety rose, they drove faster and faster. In the other car, I sensed the driver was very angry, and was indifferent about his actions.

As the two cars were driving in the tunnel, I could sense the driver chasing the other car wanted to encourage the driver in front to go ever faster, in hopes of endangering them. The driver giving chase hated these people, felt he had to give more of himself than them, that he had to work at this lousy job, while they were given everything, and he despised that. This resentment fueled his anger, motivated him to put these people in jeopardy.

In a rage of hateful emotion, he became ever more aggressive about having the other car go faster through the tunnel. The people in the front car being chased lost control of their senses, they were more interested in getting away than with their safety. In going too fast, they missed the danger ahead. Very quickly the chase turned deadly when the car in front crashed.

When the driver following noticed the accident, he thought for a moment—he did not want to be there when the authorities came to pick up the pieces. Without any remorse for the victims of this tragic accident, he drove away. I could see that this individual did not directly cause the horrific crash, but was indirectly responsible, by encouraging the other driver to go much quicker until he lost control of the vehicle.

Approximately two weeks after the dream, I was watching a news alert about princess Diana dying in a car accident. Some witnesses believed that a paparazzi was chasing their car through a tunnel before their tragic end.

Chapter Eighteen
Mental Health

When we buy a car or electronic device usually there is an operation manual. When we arrive in this world, however, we are not given such a guide. Some of us will say that the Bible or other religious text shows us the path, but at the beginning of our lives most of us rely on trial and error, and on our parents/relatives for guidance. This education varies from the culture to the region and/or country in which one lives.

I have found that in the western cultures, most of the focus is on the external body, operating our bodies efficiently by exercise, diet, and preventing disease. While I know that the body is important, I believe that we should give equal attention to the mind.

Fully believing in the phrase, "What you can't see won't hurt you," could push us away from understanding the mind, labeling something we do not see with our eyes as less important. Too much focus on the outside leaves understanding the inside at a low priority. Keeping the mind healthy deserves just as much attention as our external bodies. Similar to running a marathon to keep fit, we should be exercising our brains, and like feeding our stomach, be careful of what external emotions or ideas we digest.

Chapter Nineteen
Emotion

Our brains, as if on automatic pilot, create emotions during our experiences. I have seen how the mind, in the same way as a monkey jumps, moves around, sometimes uncontrollably. Can you recall how many thoughts/emotions you have in a day?

Emotion is energy in motion (e-motion). If that energy is not moving, we cannot send or receive emotional messages. An emotional disturbance is an emotion that causes suffering, something that is disturbing to a person or anyone who may have shared that experience. That is actually an illusion: this movement of energy sometimes affects our minds and bodies, but at its core is only energy. If we are charged up or attentive about a topic, our mental processing notes that emotion as important, whether we like that emotion or not.

You may wonder why an emotion returns, whether that energy is good, bad or indifferent to you. It is possible our response to some event, whether positive or negative, could put an importance, a mental marker on that subject. A song keeps popping into our head, or some negative experience seems to come back into our mind by itself, and sometimes it becomes annoying, as if automatic or uncontrollable. Think back to when you first developed that emotion, the great feeling you had listening to that song, or the bad memory of some incident. If our first, second, or third response to that subject is strong, the mind interprets and flags that energy as relevant enough for our mental processor to come back to. If you react to an undesirable emotion and spend time on that reoccurring memory, your mind sees that subject as still significant, and may go back several times to re-address that issue, a loop back to that emotion.

Important to remember: If not recharged (given attention), the energy (emotion) will fade in time.

An emotional feedback loop is where you interact with your emotions, making the potential for them to return. If you do not forgive yourself for something you have done, it creates an emotional loop back to that topic again. You are giving that thought importance—and the mind being a problem solver, comes back (looping around) to address that issue for further discussion. If more emotion is fed into the internal debate, that series of thoughts becomes stronger and broader. A stronger loop is formed, for instance, when a person fights or argues with an unpleasant memory, he is returning to the original thought, that is because the mind is a processor, it wants another try at working on the problem. If you stop to wrestle with an emotion, you are only making a more complex, broader one, that you may be motivated to sort out—creating a much larger emotional pathway.

I sometimes see an emotional loop after a person watches the first twenty minutes of the local evening news. He or she is bombarded with powerful doses of negativity and disturbing images. Repeatedly seeing them, a person can form an ill-conceived notion of our society. Taking that ill feeling into the mind makes us act accordingly. If you think the people in your location are unfair, criminals or corrupt, you will have ill feelings towards them, then treat them accordingly. But in behaving in that way, you could look angry, corrupt and unfair, reflecting the same image of the people you originally criticized—and there you are, back to yourself, in the creation of a negative emotional loop. Absorbing corrupt thoughts spreads anger and distaste. In that mindset, treating somebody poorly, you have reinforced the negativity that you ingested at the beginning of that emotion.

Spirits have the same emotions as we do: fear, jealously, happiness, etc. We are a combination of both physical and spiritual attributes, and some of us may display more or less. I believe we as souls need the body to become grounded, to have a place to exercise these emotions, and learn from them.

Chapter Twenty
Getting out of the Groove, Part One

Most of the time, people form patterns of thinking when experiencing something. One such pattern could be a set of instructions on how to do something ourselves. When we come back to a task, or experience an event that looks somewhat familiar, our minds fall back to that set of instructions or information to help us. Then we decide how to proceed, and most of us likely take the path of least resistance. The brain being a useful tool at optimization tries to take the mental pathway that was already used, like a familiar road.

To get out of a familiar pattern, a person must strengthen his or her own focus. A lazy mind that cannot stay on the subject will go from topic to topic, and be easily distracted by any thought that arises. To get out of the groove or set pattern of our mental conditioning, we must strengthen our focus. In meditation the mind is taught to focus on the present, not thinking about the problem a few days ago, or the challenges coming tomorrow. One-point meditation, or playing an instrument, are some ways that we can practice staying on topic or in the now.

Chapter Twenty-One
Gut Feeling

At times we can feel an emotion in our gut, the "gut feeling." Do not ignore a gut feeling that transmits danger. There have been many instances where a person has had a bad feeling, then acted upon that warning. I have seen several examples reported, such as a person avoiding an airplane flight because of a bad feeling, or avoiding an outside deck just before it falls. After that feeling of danger, an individual may not understand where it came from, feel awkward and at a loss for words, unable to explain why he or she cannot get on that amusement ride or board that airplane, only that there was a heightened sense of danger.

Chapter Twenty-Two
Messiah Consciousness/Mystic Traveler

As far back as I could remember, I was always attracted to quieting the mind, I learned later in life it was called meditation. With the goal of learning more, I spoke to a spiritually educated friend about meditation. This person explained that the ultimate or greatest goal of meditation is to reach a "Messiah Consciousness." To do that as the he said, a person must completely clear the mind and use a technique called scrying. Later in the day, I felt motivated to go to a mirror in another room.

I walked into that room which had a large mirror, the environment was not completely dark, it was dimly lit. Standing in front of the mirror I cleared my mind, focused on my eyes. As I kept focusing on my eyes, my eyes appeared closer and closer, drawn in until I journeyed inside my eyes. Then I observed a large black circle, looking very similar to a solar eclipse. As I got closer and closer to the dark circle, I entered into this black void.

In this reality I observed what looked like tiny energies/lights moving back and forth, with no clear direction—they were moving in all directions. I decided to move closer to one energy, two, perhaps three, each one had a voice, not talking, just making noise, and they felt very happy, the kind of happy feeling I have experienced being around children. As

I withdrew from these tiny energies that were moving in all sorts of directions, another energy abruptly and very excitedly appeared in front of me.

I heard the word "Messiah!"

Not being prepared to meet anyone, I replied slowly "Mike," then a few other words. Feeling confident that I must have reached the goal of a "Messiah Consciousness," I withdrew from that reality.

Back again in the room, I was standing in front of the mirror and wondered whether that spirit confirmed the goal, that I achieved the "Messiah Consciousness."

Chapter Twenty-Three
Heaven

When I was younger, like many of us, we were told there is a heaven. Could a heavenly existence be possible, where a collection of spirits is found, in another dimension or reality? While scrying, I have observed a reality filled with spirits, zipping everywhere, with not a care in the world, very happy, and without any stress.

At times, when I have been with a baby or a very young child, I have wondered if there is a connection between the spiritual reality and very young people—having an almost inherent quality of being satisfied or content. As I have observed, when in that heavenly kind of existence, spirits were very joyful being in a stress-free environment. I cannot help think that children, their spirits being in new bodies, still feel emotionally happy, in the same way they were in what some people have called heaven. The more a spirit stays in this reality, I have to feel, the more pleasurable and enlightened they become. Now when you see a child with a big smile, you may wonder sometimes as I have, whether that small person or very young animal came into this world, already having been influenced by a heavenly spiritual existence.

Chapter Twenty-Four
Concert Hall

In the 1980s, I went to a concert with some friends. Outside the building I sensed something above me, then looked up at the night sky. A spirit was warning me not to go in. The spirit told me the musicians in the band were devil worshippers. After that advice, I thought about the band, remembering they had a pentagram on one of their album covers, but I already had some suspicion they were into the occult.

Feeling no threat, I went into the building, but the spirit was not happy with my choice. While sitting down in one of seats, I noticed at least two band members being abusive to the stage assistants. My friends and I watched the concert without any problems. I would learn later, how my spirit really felt about these hateful types of people.

Chapter Twenty-Five
Black Room

One night, I had a dream about a house. In the home there is one small room, the walls were painted black. The feeling coming from this area was repulsive, as if somebody were generating hate in this dark place. Days went by and I quickly forgot about the dream.

When I was searching for a home, a real estate agent brought me to a small house. As I was going through the rooms, I quickly became alert to one that did not feel right. In approaching a small enclosure with black walls, suddenly, I remembered the dream. When I actually walked in, there was nothing special about any of the walls, but every inch of the surfaces, floor and ceiling too, were painted black. Although I could not feel any active energy, there was still a bad feeling.

I spoke to the real estate agent, letting her know about the black room, advising her that I had a bad feeling about it. She quickly went to find the owner of the home to inquire about that dark place. Without the agent requesting, the owner came over to me and apologized, saying that his relative was into devil worship and that he had problems. I told the agent that I liked the house, but the feeling in that black room prevented me from moving forward with the purchase

Chapter Twenty-Six
Witch

While searching for a meditation group, I answered an advertisement in a local newspaper for just such a group. There was a meeting scheduled almost every week. I met with the leader of the group at her home, and over several weeks I attended her guided meditations.

In between those meditation sessions, weeks later I had a dream. I could see the leader of the group and two spirits nearby, they were above her bed. She was lying there talking to the two spirits. I was told by a voice that she explored devil worship for a short time. Suddenly, she was struck by a bolt of lightning that knocked her out of the bed and onto the floor. I sensed the two spirits still above the bed were extremely frightened, immediately, they rushed away.

One evening, while meeting with the leader of the meditation group, she confided in me that she practiced wiccan. Furthermore, she admitted that she had looked into devil worship for a short time, and that it was a mistake.

I am not sure why this person, who told me she was a practicing witch, shared a recent spiritual experience with me. She explained that one night, while she was in her bedroom talking to her spirit guides, the topic of the devil worship came up. Then all of a sudden, she described, a flash of light that shot her out of bed onto the floor.

I have never been into Wiccan, and have nothing against someone practicing their own religion. I have always felt that spells were wishful thinking. If you direct or focus your mind on a wish, and choose that path with intention, your brain will, as with most other goals, put you in the right direction to that desired destination.

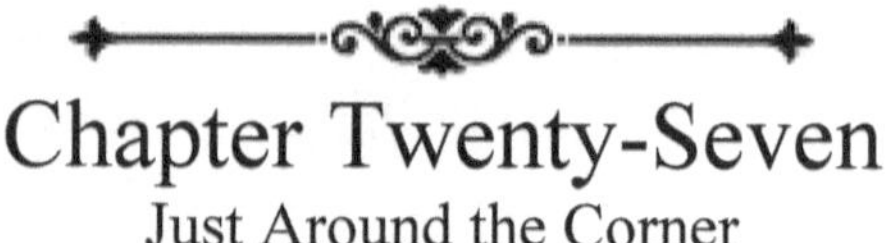

Chapter Twenty-Seven
Just Around the Corner

I was riding my bicycle one day, returning from about a thirty-mile ride. As I was about to make a right turn onto a local road, I could see a parked car on the right side of the street blocking traffic. Having this feeling something was wrong, I stopped riding. Standing there, in trying to get around this parked car, I knew someone was causing drivers to become frustrated. As I scanned the area, my head slowly turned to the right, until my eyes fixated on a man about 20-30 years old with black hair. He seemed very nervous that my eyes were directly on him, perhaps he felt guilty, as if I knew what he was doing. The feeling was nothing I had ever experienced, it was as if this person were feeding on the negative energy—that anger and frustration the drivers were having trying to avoid his car.

After his initial shock of seeing me, this person did something with his hand, and he was surprised I could see what he was doing from such a distance. His left or right hand was by his waist, fore and pinky fingers were extended while the two center fingers were folded back. This individual was very surprised I was alert to his hand gesture. From the distance that separated us, I decided the hand movement meant nothing, it was not a threat, then I started riding my bicycle past him.

Not long after the incident around the corner, I remembered a short dream that I had two weeks prior to seeing this person. In the dream, there was the car and a person standing nearby. But there was something else, a vision of police officers getting out of their car. The officer asked, "Did you park here on purpose?"

I did a little research about the hand gesture. Two people I asked said, the two out stretched fingers depicted horns, that it was the sign of the devil.

Chapter Twenty-Eight
White or Red Aura

For a very long time, if in the right state of mind, I could see auras. When my mind is calm and the light is very low, there is a possibility of seeing energy surrounding a person. In this mental state, almost waking up, between that time of consciousness and sleep—there is a possibility that anyone can see an aura, under these conditions.

I was at a gathering where there were approximately fifty people, we were sitting listening to a speaker. I did not realize I was dozing off. When I opened my eyes, everyone was still there, but I was seeing all of them with auras. They had white or red auras. Here I was seeing all of these people glowing red or white. Before this time, I could sometimes see my aura in a mirror, or another person's energy. With all these glowing images around the room, I wondered whether I was stuck seeing everyone this way. At least thirty seconds passed already, and I was still seeing everybody with auras surrounding their bodies. After almost a minute, the auras disappeared. I wondered why I was seeing auras in different colors, with this number of people. Almost half of them were seen as either white or red.

A few days later I had a very brief dream, one of those dreams which seemed real. A spirit asked me a question, "What should happen to the bad ones?"

Without thinking, I said "Aneurysm," then "Blood clot."

When I realized what I said, and what was being asked, and before I could withdraw what I said, the dream ended. When I woke up, I realized the spirit was referring to the people with the red auras.

Chapter Twenty-Nine
The Thief of Amsterdam

I was walking in Amsterdam with a friend. Since he was a retired police officer, I thought my friend would be more alert to his surroundings. At the time, I was walking with a moderately-priced digital camera. The street we were on had very few people, and I thought two good-sized guys like us could take care of ourselves, if need be. All of a sudden, I sensed something that needed my attention. I turned to my left flank to see a man standing across the street eager to make some kind of move. I made sure in that brief moment to make eye contact, to let this person know I knew of his presence and that he lost the element of surprise. Thinking that he got the message, I told my friend that we were being watched, to stay alert, and we kept walking.

As we were moving along to the next street, I had the feeling that this person was not done. Again, I turned my head and made eye contact with him for the second time, this time motioning my head in a way that told him, it is time to move on. Thinking that he received the non-verbal message again, we continued to walk to a more populated street with shops, and there was no incident.

After about ten minutes, we came upon a small crowd of people gathered near a man being arrested. I noticed that this suspect was the same man I warned earlier. While being held in custody, he could not stop staring at me, although the officer was pulling on him. I pointed out to my friend that he was the person whom I had warned him about, several minutes earlier. We were about 15 meters/fifty feet away from the arresting officer, and I did not know what to say to this individual being arrested, who I assume was a thief.

I quietly said to my friend, "Let's go."

As we were walking away, I did not think of him as evil or that he deserved what he got, I thought this may be a new beginning for him, if he follows the right path.

While walking away from the arrest, I remembered something in a dream about the surroundings I was seeing. In the dream, a person's path was changed. He did not expect what was coming and was not able to control what was about to happen to him, as if he were being punished. Then the dream ended. I had to wonder if this vision was related to meeting this thief of Amsterdam.

Chapter Thirty
Horsing Around

I had a very short dream where I observed a horse inside a barn, a spirit was able to control this animal. It seemed the horse was very shocked, something aroused its attention, then the spirit rendered the animal motionless.

Two weeks later, I was visiting a friend around the holidays, and he told me that he was going to light some fireworks. After having seen displays of fireworks plenty of times, I decided to take a relaxing walk around the property instead.

As I was walking around the house, I discovered a small building. As I crossed the doorway, I started hearing the fireworks. Inside the structure was a stall with hay scattered around the floor. Through the dark, I could see a horse charging at me. Then abruptly, the horse stopped. The horse went from a highly frightened creature to a very passive animal, all going on within a second or two. Although I was angry with my friend, who should have known better than to scare this poor horse with the fireworks, I decided to move closer. Without knowing me, he allowed me to pet him. It almost felt we became friends instantly. A few minutes later, feeling that the horse calmed down enough, I returned to my friends, still annoyed with my friend for scaring this animal.

Chapter Thirty-One
Saying Goodbye to Mother

Approximately three months before my mother passed, I had what I thought was a dream. In the first part, I watched my mother's spirit viewing her corpse on a bed. She was listening attentively, and there was an image of me standing beside her lifeless body. I looked down at her saying "I love you," and then I felt extreme happiness from her spirit. In the next part of the dream, this time in black and white, there was an image of a small lion on each side of her month, pushing her lips up into a smile.

I forgot about the dream until three months later. After a full night of sleeping, in the early morning, being half asleep, I heard a voice.

A female voice said, "What do you think of her?"

I knew she was asking about my mother. I said in a half-conscious state of mind, with a slow voice, "Very good."

Then she asked another question, "Should she go slow or fast?"

Again, in a sleepy voice I said, "Fast."

After waking up, I realized that short conversation relating to my mother was about her death.

Two weeks later, my mother died very quickly due to a heart problem. I went into her room where she was lying. Standing beside her, I looked down at her blank face and said, "I love you."

Suddenly her face changed, no one was touching her, and she was lifeless. Instead of the distressed blank face that was there, I could see she was smiling, with that beautiful smile she always had. I was not shocked that her face changed; the smile did not cheer me up like it sometimes did when she was alive. When I came back a half hour later the smile was gone. I realized my mother had earlier sent me a message with that facial expression.

In the three months after she died, I had three short encounters with her spirit. In two of them, she was with a female spirit. It seemed as though this other soul was guiding her though moments in her past life and into the present. When these two spirits recognized that I could see them, they disappeared as quickly as they came in.

One night about ten weeks after she died, I was sleeping in my bed. A feeling came over me, that same feeling I had with her when I was a child. I embraced that feeling, knowing it was from her, and sent my feeling of love back to her. I knew that might be the last time I would sense her, that she was saying goodbye.

After that night, I remembered an experience when I was a child. I was about five years old, lying on a couch or bed, and my mother was looking straight down at me. I could sense her affection or love. At that time, in a child's body, looking up at her I thought, what a beautiful woman. Then out of nowhere, an angry female voice said, "You will only have this feeling one more time."

I did not understand then what this spirit meant, that is until a few short months after my mother passed. That is when my mother sent me that one last message. When I was about to go to retire for the night, I knew my mother's spirit was above my bed. She was transmitting that same feeling of love, the same kind of sensation she had felt for me, when she looked down at me as a child; this was that last feeling the spirit had told me about a long time ago.

Chapter Thirty-Two
Saying Goodbye to Father

My father's passing was very uneventful. I was very annoyed with his behavior. He had a very severe clinical depression with some nasty side effects. I did not want to see him during the transition out of his body to the spiritual reality. I was afraid that my being angry with him would be of no benefit, knowing that his behavior was related to mental illness. I was very supportive and did not show most of my disapproval at his condition—the negative state of mind which affected his behavior and that he had no desire to change.

Although I did not wish to see his spirit, he did communicate with me. He was very weak the day he died. During a brief time outside of his home, I had a feeling from him only for a few seconds. It was a sensation of liberation and freedom. When I came back to check on him, I found his body. I thought about that feeling he transmitted; he was freed from the physical and mental suffering, especially from the psychological despair. At the time, I did not know what became of my father's soul after that communication, but I did wish him luck and hope for the path he may choose.

Chapter Thirty-Three
Hell

There is no Hell, not in the way you may have been educated. I believe the concept of Hell was derived from the basic scheme of opposites, such as dark or light, cold or hot, and Heaven or Hell. The idea of a demonic reality has been used for centuries to scare the population, a sinister fairy tale. If we are bad, we are sometimes warned that we are going to Hell. Some religious media personalities have taken the concept of Hell and used it for their own political and/or economic agenda, and know all too well how to generate fear, as used for generations to control the masses.

We may have been told that this fiery underworld is occupied by Satan, agents of evil, and that the soul who goes there is tortured for his sins. This idea of Hell is not a fictional place of suffering, fire and darkness, it is more of a feeling.

You may feel as if you are in Hell sometimes, but it is not any type of spiritual Hell. When I think of a spirit eventually being sent to Hell, I see that soul being put back here in this reality to feel, and perhaps experience in some way the injustice of past actions.

There is a possibility that a spirit could be punished, made to feel what the victim had felt. This seems simple enough, but think about a mass murderer, such as Adolf Hitler. Perhaps his spirit was made to feel a multitude of harsh sensations, the very suffering he was responsible for committing: the feeling in his gut of starvation, the effect of choking on poison gas, the shattering of metal ripping through the body from a bullet or shrapnel, burning flesh from a fire, or the despair of losing a child or spouse. Being put in a similar environment to feel the same negative outcomes of your actions is the real Hell. Sharing the pain of the victim may not be the final punishment. A spirit who does not behave like a human may not return as one.

Chapter Thirty-Four
God

It is completely possible that a very powerful spirit whom some have witnessed, and have named God, could create planetary conditions on a level where life could thrive. With the proper combination of natural attributes: air, water, sea, temperature, and others—life is supported.

The environmental damage we are seeing presently is an un-doing of the natural process. Whether or not God had any influence on the development of this world, damaging this planet is disrespectful to your home, human beings, other life, and maybe God.

The earth is a living entity inhabited by other living things. We all share the responsibility of maintaining and respecting this world. When the astronauts looked back at the earth, some could not help see and think that this is one world without fences or borders.

I believe a very powerful spirit does exist.

I have watched interviews with atheists, and have to say their message was reasonable—you believe what you can see, what is logical and predictable in our world. I do have to admit that I declared myself an atheist for a short time. I went almost a decade without any spiritual experience, and the answer to the question of whether God had any influence on us seemed more distant. Spirituality was moved more to the back of my mind; the idea of God and spirits faded into my distant memory. For perhaps a year, I could not recall those experiences and remained an atheist. Then I reminded myself about my very first memory where I thanked a spirit who was named God, that there is a very powerful spirit out there. In time, I could not deny that childhood memory of an incredibly strong spirit.

During my short time with this very powerful spirit, I could not help but feel the immense energy—the kind of energy that could scare another spirit into attentive caution. I am not sure I can describe the feeling in words, but will try. Imagine you are surrounded by twelve high-powered diesel locomotives, all accelerating at top engine speed with a heavy load to pull, but they are not moving anywhere. You can hear and see these powerful engines. Now remove what your eyes could see, then the sound. You now have only that incredible powerful raw sensation or vibration.

You may ask, "What can this powerful spirit do?" The answer is simply change reality, and under that condition, the possibilities are enormous. When I say change reality, any life or path can be changed, and the future can be altered before it becomes reality to you. Life builds on the options available in that reality. This powerful conscious energy flows in a way that is open to all the possibilities, the way water flows in any direction.

From my spiritual experiences, I know that God and other spirits or guides are actively affecting us all. In your experiences, you may have been aware of a slight change, for a brief moment, as if something felt strangely different. These kinds of changes can sometimes occur without our knowledge. Almost mysteriously, some of us may have felt a tiny hint of them, that there was possibly something there.

If you are wondering whether God can change the weather, as I have said, this spirit can change our reality, and the weather is within the scope of our reality—of course, the answer is yes.

God is not everywhere, which is a classic assumption. While I believe it is wrong to say God is with us all the time, it is correct to say that God can be anywhere and know everything.

You may have heard that your life flashes before your eyes when you die. Everything we see, smell, hear, feel and experience is stored in our human memory. All this information is a collection available to us throughout life, and when our bodies expire, that memory is still available to us and to our spiritual helpers. Our information, the summation of experiences and actions, guides us to our ultimate destination. I believe God can judge a person very quickly, without someone's knowledge, then be on to the next life. Similar to a court, the truth/evidence of this life, our collective memory of feelings and events is plain to see, and judged accordingly. Perhaps the next destination is a long stay in spiritual reality (heaven) or moving on to another life (in a good or hellish type of environment).

The spirit of God may be feared by other spirits. Any spirit would be more alert when standing with this intense energy, keep attentive, and move away in great fear if this powerful entity were angry. God, being at a higher level, can observe a spirit without its knowledge, and that is still true if that soul is able to sense other spirits.

I inform people, especially when they are at risk of an undesirable judgement, "What do you want to see at the end of your life?" I say the choice is yours now, and although you may have already made an error, the spiritual world does see your efforts in understanding a mistake, correcting it, and avoiding that mistake in the future. I believe our main spiritual goal is to learn, and since we are subject to the human condition, we do not always have a smooth path to that outcome. The unfortunate part of our lifetime of education, of being human, is to learn by some of our mistakes.

Chapter Thirty-Five
Suicide

If you were given a life by God, would it be an insult to that great spirit to take that life, to destroy his creation? Unless someone is gravely ill, I believe suicide disrespects the value of any life. In deciding the next life chosen, there may be a risk involved in killing yourself, in devaluing what you were given. That devaluation may affect what form you take in the next life.

There have been many reports of mass shootings. For a person committing suicide who kills others, I cannot imagine the feeling the murderer will have after his spirit leaves the confines of his body. This type of person may be angry at certain people, or at the world, before ending his or her life, he may believe that the best revenge for difficult circumstances is to kill other individuals. When the spirit of the killer leaves his body, those of the departed are there too, in the same room or environment. Imagine one or more spirits who are probably very annoyed, the embarrassment of confronting them, and the realization that there is a spiritual penalty for such a crime. The murderer may think that by suicide, he can abandon the responsibility or punishment in this reality, only to find several angry spirits, and the ultimate judgment of his life's journey awaiting him. I believe the criminal sentence in this reality, if there is no death penalty, is better than the destination the murderer's soul goes to once he has departed his physical body.

Chapter Thirty-Six
Bookstore

In a dream, another spirit and I were observing the inside of a bookstore. I thought the other spirit, a male, had a similar ability in that we were at the same location as spirits—outside our bodies; but there was a difference. His spirit was below me, and while I could see him, he did not know I was there.

When I say below me, I do not say that in a derogatory way. If you are looking at a wall, my spirit was near the ceiling, and his appeared closer to the middle section of the wall. He had no idea that I was observing him from above. About two weeks later, I was at the same bookstore that I had seen in the dream, seeing the same person from the vision—he had no clue I knew of his ability.

Chapter Thirty-Seven
My Spirit

I was visiting a very good friend. We were in her living room when we heard a loud noise, and I was sensing a spirit. When I looked up near the ceiling, I could see a white cloud. In the middle of the cloud was what looked like a very bright white light, a shining silver/white color.

I told my friend there was a spirit in the room, and not to fear, that I was not sensing any threat. A few seconds later, we heard a second loud sound. Although the noise was loud, nothing moved or fell down. She seemed a little unnerved by the strange occurrence, but she said there was no problem.

As I was leaving her home, walking to the parking lot, I stopped abruptly, standing there near my car. A memory started to come back, triggered by seeing my car parked.

Approximately two weeks prior to meeting her, while sleeping, I had seen my car parked in this same lane. Not only that, I recalled other parts of the vision. One was a desire to see my spirit, to see what I looked like in that form; the other was whether or not my spirit can make sounds. As if my spirit had granted my wish or helped with my curiously, I now know how I appear in spiritual color and shape. After seeing my spirit, I understand better that we are not just alive in these bodies, we are all spiritual life-forms.

Chapter Thirty-Eight
Losing my Fiancé

In a dream about my fiancé, there was a large room with a casket. I could see myself standing in front of the coffin, looking down seeing her lifeless body with her eyes closed. In the room, in the space above my physical body, was the spirit of my fiancé looking down at me standing next to her dead body lying there. My spirit made my physical body in the dream move to her, then gently kiss her goodbye. Looking at her spirit below mine, although she could not see or detect my spirit, she became extremely happy. That kiss made her feel she was really loved in that moment—something that made her life feel gratified or more complete. She stayed in that moment maybe too long, when there was a loud sound. A male voice yelled out her name, then realizing she had to go, her spirit disappeared.

Approximately three months after this dream, my fiancé died. When she was still alive, I remembered the dream, then tried to help improve her health. I told her how important it was to work at getting better. Ultimately, she could not recover from this illness.

At her funeral, I was not thinking about the dream, I was in grief, only remembering the visions of her death shortly after an impulse came to me, to bend down to kiss her goodbye. And, at times, recalling my memories of the funeral, I felt she was given the appropriate farewell. With the understanding that only her body died, I knew she was somewhere else now.

Chapter Thirty-Nine
My Favorite Cousin

I had a cousin whom I enjoyed visiting as a child. He was a kind gentleman that I always looked forward to meeting. I had a series of dreams/visions three months prior to his leaving this world. The first was an image of a room in a building, the walls appeared yellow and/or brown. There were two family members in a hallway arguing about someone—I knew it was about their father and how to proceed with his healthcare.

In the next set of visions, I could see my cousin's spirit after having left his body, and another soul waiting to meet him. The first thing my cousin did was to transmit his desire to see his wife. The other spirit was very surprised at his insistence, told my cousin that he was not in a position to make demands. In his life, my cousin was wealthy and was used to getting what he wanted. I approached the two of them. Noticing my presence, the spirit with him kept very quiet while my cousin still insisted on seeing his spouse. In observing other spirits leave this world, they usually go back to look at parts of their lives, and I felt he should proceed in the same way. I expressed my wish to the spirit next to him that he should see his family. My cousin refused. I said to this helper spirit by his side, he should be convinced, and without any questions asked, both of them disappeared.

When I returned to the two spirits in another vision a day or two later, I could tell my cousin was very receptive now, he was ready to revisit his family. Then my cousin asked the soul with him who I was. When told, his reaction was a surprise, almost denial. Because I liked my relative, I told the spirit next to him that he was a hard-working family man.

Knowing that he was ready to see his family, we were suddenly in a large room, and there was his son standing at a podium, speaking to an audience about his father. My cousin had several sons and a daughter, but he was closest to this son and wanted to see him first—the child who was taking care of him. He did observe several other sons and family members, but was still eager to meet with his wife again. After having seen his family, he was unhappy to learn there were other memories from his life he needed to confront. I could sense that he did not like the idea of seeing how he treated other lives, whether they were human or other species. He may have learned at that moment that we are not judged on how much money we have; we are judged on how we treated living things.

Before departing, my cousin wanted me to transmit a message. He asked if I could tell his son that he was alright. That was the first time a spirit wanted me to send a message, and I accepted.

When my cousin died, based on the visions I had about him, I knew there was a good chance of seeing him at the funeral. In a large room at the funeral home, his son was speaking. In the dream, he was watching his son for what seemed about five minutes. But in my human body, seeing his family at the funeral in our reality, I observed what looked like a spark of energy near the ceiling, for what seemed about five seconds. Shortly after that, I had a new understanding. In one reality, he was there for a few seconds; in the other, he was there for what seemed about five minutes; leaving me wonder if one reality moves at a different rate of speed than the other.

Chapter Forty
Mystic Sex, Part One

While sleeping at a hotel in Washington, D.C., in the mid 1990s, I had a strange dream. I was in the room of a beautiful woman with long black hair. She was asked about her sexual fantasy, then suddenly there she was, wearing a sexy outfit of her own choosing. After she made her choice, I could remember observing her having sex with an image of me. In the morning upon waking up, I thought, what a nice dream.

While getting ready to leave the hotel, standing in the lobby a short distance away, was a beautiful woman with long black hair. When she finally turned her head—she was slightly startled when her eyes met mine. I started to think, that was her from the dream, and her eyes stayed fixed on mine. For a moment I thought it was only a dream. But then every few minutes we found ourselves staring at each other. Perhaps she was wondering the same thing I was, is that the person from the dream? I thought about asking if we had met before, or just giving her my phone number to ask questions, to sort this out later. This situation was very strange and my ride had arrived, but there she was again, this time outside the hotel looking at me, perhaps waiting for me to talk to her, before driving away in the cab.

While I was debating in my mind as to whether the dream was real and what to do, the cab pulled away from the curb. I have always wondered about that dream; was it a dream or a vision. If that was really her while I was sleeping, did she ever forget, does she wonder about that guy she met in a dream?

Chapter Forty-One
9/11

During the two years prior to the 9/11 tragedy, I was having bad dreams. At one point, I went to my doctor to see if they could be stopped, they were nightmares I could not imagine. I told the physician that in the past I would have a dream, then see those same scenes at a later date. After meeting with my doctor, he said, "Let me talk to my colleague and I'll get back to you."

A few days later we spoke again. He said that there was nothing that could be done, that whatever I have is natural, and it should not be stopped, similar to an early warning system.

In one of the dreams, a man is sitting at a desk. Behind him is a twin-engine jet coming towards the window—he had no clue what was about to happen. And in another dream, I sensed the grief, desperation and utter terror when people decided to either jump out of a window, or off a roof to avoid the flames.

In one more dream that was longer, I sensed that a good soul did not belong there, as he was falling down from the tall building. Immediately, I traveled down with this person, keeping him from screaming, until the end—upon the release of his soul from his body. I felt his end was more dignified in this way.

In one vision, I had seen something that seemed amazing, as a building fell apart. After what looked as if large rocks were falling down, there was a lone survivor. I wondered if that person's spirit knew of the right place and time to be.

These dreams brought back a memory I had as a child. I remembered playing with a small toy airplane, and there was a picture of the World Trade Center in New York. As a child, with the model in my hand, I was making believe the plane was flying. Without thinking my arm went in the direction of the building. Although I could have imagined the airplane going in any direction, my hand went toward the picture containing the building. I crashed my toy airplane into the World Trade Center photo, then my eyes went blank. All I could see was white, almost as if snow were falling down, and what looked like snow drifts in the street. Now that I look back on it, the white powder could have represented the ash falling down and collecting in the streets, that is after the twin tower buildings came crashing down.

Chapter Forty-Two
Reincarnation

I have to believe in reincarnation, that is because I am an old soul. I have seen male and female spirits, and have occasionally wondered if there could be spiritual placement errors. What may hint of that is when I have heard a little boy say, I am really a girl, or the opposite, a little girl saying I am really a boy.

Reincarnation may not only occur with human bodies; other species could experience spiritual transitions.

Chapter Forty-Three
Strange Trip

I had agreed with friends to go on a trip to a beach resort town for a few days. I was not sure at the time why I imagined children and adults switching roles. Perhaps I was influenced by a news report about parents fighting with one another, behaving like children at a baseball game for kids. I was imaging a few adults and children standing together, with the kids behaving as adults and the grownups acting like children. Upon arrival at the beach town, in front of the hotel, were two adults standing next to two children. Strangely enough, the two kids were standing quietly; appearing mature while the adults were fighting like children. I wondered if there were some type of coincidence, what I imagined, inspired by the news report, was being demonstrated in front of me.

While at the beach I went into the ocean to swim. About 50 feet away in the deeper water was some activity, it was not the movement of people. I could see small fins moving around, and felt something positive. As I moved closer, I could see that there were approximately three dolphins trying to get my attention. But then I heard somebody on the shore yell, "Shark!"

I thought to myself, "How disrespectful to these creatures?"

By saying shark, this person without confirming what these animals were, recklessly put these dolphins in danger. To keep attention away from these friendly creatures, I decided to swim back to the shore. If nobody were in the water, the authorities would not see a safety threat, and these creatures could escape any potential danger to their lives.

Chapter Forty-Four
Health Care Providers/SARS-CoV-2

During the Covid 19 crisis, I have seen how people have embraced the first responders and healthcare providers. They have called them heroes and heroines, and while I find that type of recognition admirable, what I have actually felt regarding this praise is far from congratulatory. Several of these people, not knowing what I am sensing, are apprehensive about meeting with a doctor or nurse. They are afraid of these first responders and medical providers, fearing that they are going to spread the disease to them. Other individuals who were more centered on themselves, I felt were thinking "Better you than me." Fear brings about many side effects, not always pleasant to those of us who can sense this type of emotion.

Chapter Forty-Five
Goldie

Goldie was an English Mastiff, and I met her at the door of a home. Because of her size, loud barking and jumping up and down, she scared most people approaching the house. When coming up to her at the front door, her reaction was a surprise. Within a second, I had to decide to run or fight (fight or flight) from this dog I thought was threatening me. I was thinking in that second or two, I am too close and if I run she will catch me, therefore, I decided to take a stand. I reacted by standing sideways, arms up in a fighting position, eyes focused on her. All of a sudden, she stopped jumping around, having a look of surprise, she seemed shocked; she was standing still, somewhat confused. It seemed as if she was in a situation she was not used to. Probably in her mind, she remembered how the majority of people ran away from her aggressive behavior. Here I was in a fighting stance, and she was frozen. After a few seconds, she became frightened and started to walk away. Realizing that she was not a crazy animal, just a smart dog guarding a home, intimidating and chasing away any unsuspecting individuals with her size and ferocity.

As a result of this abrupt meeting, I felt that if I did not console her she could be harmed mentally by the fear she felt after our confrontation. I walked closer, held my hand under her mouth, to show her I was not a threat. She was still afraid, and approached my hand slowly. Once she felt comfortable, she bowed down. Perhaps she expected me to reprimand or strike her for her prior behavior. I did not hurt this beautiful creature. She stood up, licked/kissed my hand. Suddenly, we were friends. I have to guess going forward, she probably thought twice about scaring people at the front door again.

Chapter Forty-Six
Animals

In my experience with meeting dogs, cats and other animals for the first time, eventually, most of them walk up to me, and we become friends. I have received feedback from some of their owners, "My cat or dog does not go to anyone, but they go to you."

A few pet owners I have met have said, when people come to my home, my pet is the best judge of character. One person said, "Since my dog likes you, you're okay with me."

Then I said with a smile," I must have passed the test."

I believe, in the same way animals have a heighted sense of sound, smell and eyesight, these dogs, cats and other animals can sense people, whether they have fear, compassion, or some raw feeling, such as a positive or negative aura. An animal may have an easier time approaching you for the first time if they sense a positive kind of person, one they perceive as presenting very little danger to themselves and their caretaker.

Chapter Forty-Seven
You Cannot Change the Past

B ack in the mid 1990s, I was watching a show about a killing that occurred in the state of Florida, United States. Something about this crime did not seem right, and I could not identify what it was at that time.

I pondered the legal case for a week or two, then one night had a dream relating to the crime. I could see a wet area with many long weeds/plants growing, and a clearing with a small group of people sitting together. I sensed they were planning revenge against somebody. In the actual crime, some people were accused of planning the murder. Apparently, I was seeing the past. In this dream, I was observing this set of people talk about planning a crime. But there was something else; they all agreed to put this plan on hold. One person had more anger than the others in the group. Also, he was going to initiate the crime without anyone else's knowing, a betrayal of their agreement to put the revenge on hold.

Knowing that I could not remain in the past, I found myself traveling back to the present; I was on some kind of pathway connecting these places. Since I gained the knowledge that only one person in this group was really guilty, I thought, maybe I could go back and change something to alter the past. Then very quickly, I had the most sickening feeling in my gut, a nauseating impulse to halt what I was considering, that it would create more problems than it would solve. This horrible feeling in my stomach was similar to the sensation I felt when Trump became the U.S. president.

After this dream, I wondered what would happen if someone were to go back in time to change things, the possible repercussions to the present. I concluded that the past should not be changed, because it could possibly undo or loosen the fabric of our reality. The material or energy keeping this reality stable could unravel. Changing the past could alter the chain of events leading to the creation of your life or others. For the mystic traveler who wants to avoid an undesirable outcome or disaster, the past must only be observed and not disturbed, that is when traveling on an astral plane.

Chapter Forty-Eight
Trump

When I first started listening to Trump, I did it with some hesitation because he reminded me of a friend I used to know. This person I knew and observed was somewhat of a con-man, a hustler. He told people what they wanted to hear. I thought about his sales pitch, "Make America great again." I know Americans want to hear that. Using some critical thinking, that must imply America is not great now. The pitch did not make sense, because I thought of America as already having the greatest of potential.

I became very concerned after the 2016 American election for President. I asked a friend whom he voted for, he answered, "Trump."

My response to him without thinking was, "You voted for the anti-Christ."

I thought, I usually do not speak spontaneously in this way, and that had me thinking, could my reaction simply be a gut feeling?

When Trump boasted that he could kill somebody on a street in New York and his supporters would still cheer for him, I felt he was indirectly insulting them, thinking of them as mindless followers. Then I wondered, could he be a sociopath?

Back in 2016, I read a report about a letter sent to the United States Congress regarding Trump. In the letter, over 200 psychiatric healthcare professionals warned that Trump was unstable, a narcissist and sociopath, and a danger to national security. You could label him a conman, liar or anything else, but having knowledge of this letter, I could see how his symptoms were related to mental illness. Compulsive lying is noted in sociopaths, and then I read an article about how a newspaper was keeping an average daily number, as to how many lies he committed each day.

Trump once said he was a stable genius. That had me laughing, reminding me of a cartoon I once watched with a coyote who called himself a genius. If you have ever watched this cartoon character, you know what becomes of the genius at the end of every episode.

I believe that a person cannot hide his real self forever. The energy to keep the lock on his inner thoughts cannot stay closed all the time; like any muscle, it must rest, open when the mental muscle contracts then relaxes. After watching Trump on television, I observed a strange omen: he held the Bible in his hand upside down. I wondered, was that one of those moments when this life form revealed his inner core—the part of us that cannot filter out every possible emotion, the energy that is natural and integral to us, and part of our upbringing. When I ponder whether I accidentally called him the anti-Christ in 2016, I have wondered about seeing him hold the Bible upside down. I cannot help but think this incident could be one of those moments, an opportunity to see a sign, when the mental lock is open exposing his inner core.

Chapter Forty-Nine
The War Criminal

Several years ago, I was watching a show about hunting World War II Nazis. In the episode, there was a scene in which an airplane crashed into a lake. It was suspected that a war criminal had been flying on that plane, presumed to be running away from capture.

For a few days after the episode, I thought about the crash. Did the occupants in that aircraft survive, and if they did not, what would happen to the spirit of this war criminal?

Then one night, not too long after the show broadcast, I had a dream about that same plane. I was seeing an old twin-engine airplane in a lake, and could sense that possibly something spiritual was about to occur. A spirit appeared above the aircraft, very quickly grabbing one of the spirits involved in the crash. There was no discussion, no bargaining. The soul who was just liberated from his body was aggressively pulled away to some other place.

In comparison to other visions I have had about souls who had left their bodies, at the first encounter with a helper spirit, there was respect, a discussion or greeting. This entity departing the airplane was not given any such courtesy, in the same way that other souls were treated. I do not know where this spirit was taken, but I have to imagine that if he were a war criminal, he did not go to a heavenly destination.

Chapter Fifty
The Man on the Moon

I have sometimes wondered whether a very powerful ancient spirit put the image of a man on the moon. What if in the dark of night, a spirit expecting us to look at the sky wanted us to know we were not alone, or to remind us of our humanity? Scientists like to explain away such geological images as ancient volcanic shifts in land masses, but a spirit as powerful as God could have easily left us a message. Is it coincidence that this image is in the right location for all of us to view in the night sky, and could this face/symbol represent a message to all of us? Think about it, everyone in this world will one day look up at the moon and wonder.

Chapter Fifty-One
Castles

I believe that castles are still being built today, but not with the customary structure and appearance of high walls and towers made of stone and brick. Castles traditionally had a collection of people who belonged to the kingdom. The hierarchy included a king and/or a queen, some senior officials, and the subjects who served them.

Individuals who lacked the power and wealth were expected to work harder than those at the top of the royal classes. The lower classes did the dirty jobs, kept the realm maintained, spent more energy to have the basic necessities, and did not share in the good health and prosperity.

Kingdoms of the past are similar in many ways to the framework of corporations today. Starting from the outside, surrounding many castles is a protective barrier, sometimes with a small stream of water, and an army of soldiers ready to fight all invaders. Most corporations are surrounded by fences/walls, with an army of security forces. Instead of the outdated look-out towers and moats containing man-eating animals, there are modern methods used as barriers, such as cameras, electrified fences and electronic firewalls.

Instead of a king or queen controlling the kingdom and their officials, a corporation has a CEO, president and officers under them. In the same way riches went only to a select few people, where the kings and inner circle kept most of the wealth, there are CEOs, board members and excusive members/investors who retain most of the riches. The lower classes are told if they work hard, they might attain more wealth and join this exclusive group. Meanwhile, they still suffer to maintain a type of system which consists of a class hierarchy, security forces and economy.

Chapter Fifty-Two
Planet Earth

Whether you believe God created this world or assisted in the development of an environment that supports life, I doubt he likes the current path. When I say assist, I have sometimes wondered whether God observed a planet that could almost support life, then added something to allow living organisms to thrive. For instance, what if he created the magnetic field around the earth? Without it, our sun's radiation would kill everything. What if God had an effect on our planetary orbit? A planet orbiting too far from its star would be too cold to support most life, if closer to its star, the temperature could be as high as that on the planet Venus, a hellish environment of heat and greenhouse gases. Presently, the earth is in an ideal circular orbit that supports a very large biodiversity.

Like a doctor who performs a delicate and skillful procedure, he takes pride in his work. I believe those of us allowing this world to die an environmental death are undermining the work that has been done; the inaction to correct the situation is reckless and irresponsible. My message to the oil companies, polluters and enablers, "You don't take the profits with you, and you could be held accountable in another type of court, the spiritual kind."

Chapter Fifty-Three
The Message

If sometimes we had a better guide book to life, we would not have to learn by our mistakes, or we could minimize them. While we are out in the world, we have to rely on our senses, not just our intellect, and with that we should expect some surprises, where is the fun without the mystery?

Remember, they want to see what you do with this life. As long as you are living, you could make that outcome positive—to have that memory for later. You have that kind of control, a kind of memory storage or collection you are responsible for. When you are looking back at this life, you will see those moments—you sometimes have the opportunity while living to choose and/or make your new memories, to fill that collection.

The spirit is eternal and records a lifetime of events, best to control the course of that. You may have heard of the phrase "What comes around, goes around." Furthermore, you may have heard something similar to this: best to control what comes around now, or it could hurt you in the end.

Although you have read about a series of messages based on my experiences, my message to you: there is a positive force who could help, and for those of you in the know, the theft in the night is active.

About the Author

Although I am not religious, I have had spiritual and mystical experiences since being a child. I am a board-certified healthcare provider who has worked on the front-line during the pandemic crisis.